People of the Bible

The Bible through stories and pictures

Joseph the Dream Teller

Copyright © in this format Belitha Press Ltd, 1984

Text copyright © Catherine Storr 1984

Illustrations copyright © Chris Molan 1984

Art Director: Treld Bicknell

First published in Great Britain in paperback 1984
by Methuen Children's Books Ltd,
11 New Fetter Lane, London EC4P 4EE

Conceived, designed and produced by Belitha Press Ltd,
40 Belitha Villas, London N1 1PD

ISBN 0 416 47030 0

Printed in Hong Kong
by South China Printing Co

All rights reserved. No part of this book may be
reproduced or utilized in any form or by any means,
electronic or mechanical, including photocopying,
recording, or by any information storage and
retrieval system, without permission in writing
from the Publisher.

Joseph the Dream Teller

Retold by Catherine Storr
Pictures by Chris Molan

Methuen Children's Books
in association with Belitha Press Ltd

After Joseph's brothers had sold him
to some travelling merchants,
he was taken from Canaan down to Egypt.
It was a long dusty journey.
There the merchants sold him to Potiphar,
one of the officers of Pharaoh, the King.

Joseph was clever
and everything he was given to do went well.
When Potiphar saw this,
he made Joseph the overseer in his house.
Everything that Potiphar had
was looked after by Joseph.
Potiphar trusted him with all his possessions.

Joseph was a very good-looking young man.
Potiphar's wife saw him and liked him.
She said to Joseph, 'I love you!'

But Joseph said, 'My master, your husband, has trusted me with everything he has. It would be very wicked of me to love you.'

Potiphar's wife waited until she and Joseph
were alone in the house.
Then she caught hold of his coat and said,
'Stay here with me!' But he ran away,
leaving his coat in her hand. She was furious.
She said to Potiphar,
'Your Hebrew servant has insulted me.'

When he heard this, Potiphar was very angry.
He sent Joseph to the prison
where the King's prisoners were kept.
There the prison governor trusted him.
He let him look after the other prisoners.

Soon after this, Pharaoh the King was angry
with his chief butler and with his chief baker.
They were both sent to prison,
where Joseph looked after them.
One night each of them dreamed a dream.
The next morning they were both sad.

Joseph asked them, 'Why are you so sad?'
Then they told him their dreams.
The butler said, 'I dreamed I saw a vine
with three branches.
Then I saw buds, and blossoms,
and the ripe grapes. I took the grapes
and pressed them into Pharaoh's cup.
Then I put the cup into Pharaoh's hand.'

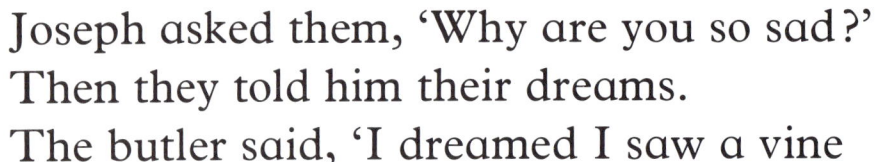

Joseph said, 'The three branches are three days.
Three days from now
Pharaoh will take you back into his palace
and you will hand him his cup of wine
just as you used to. When this happens,
please remember I'm here in prison,
and try to get me out
for I have done nothing wrong.'

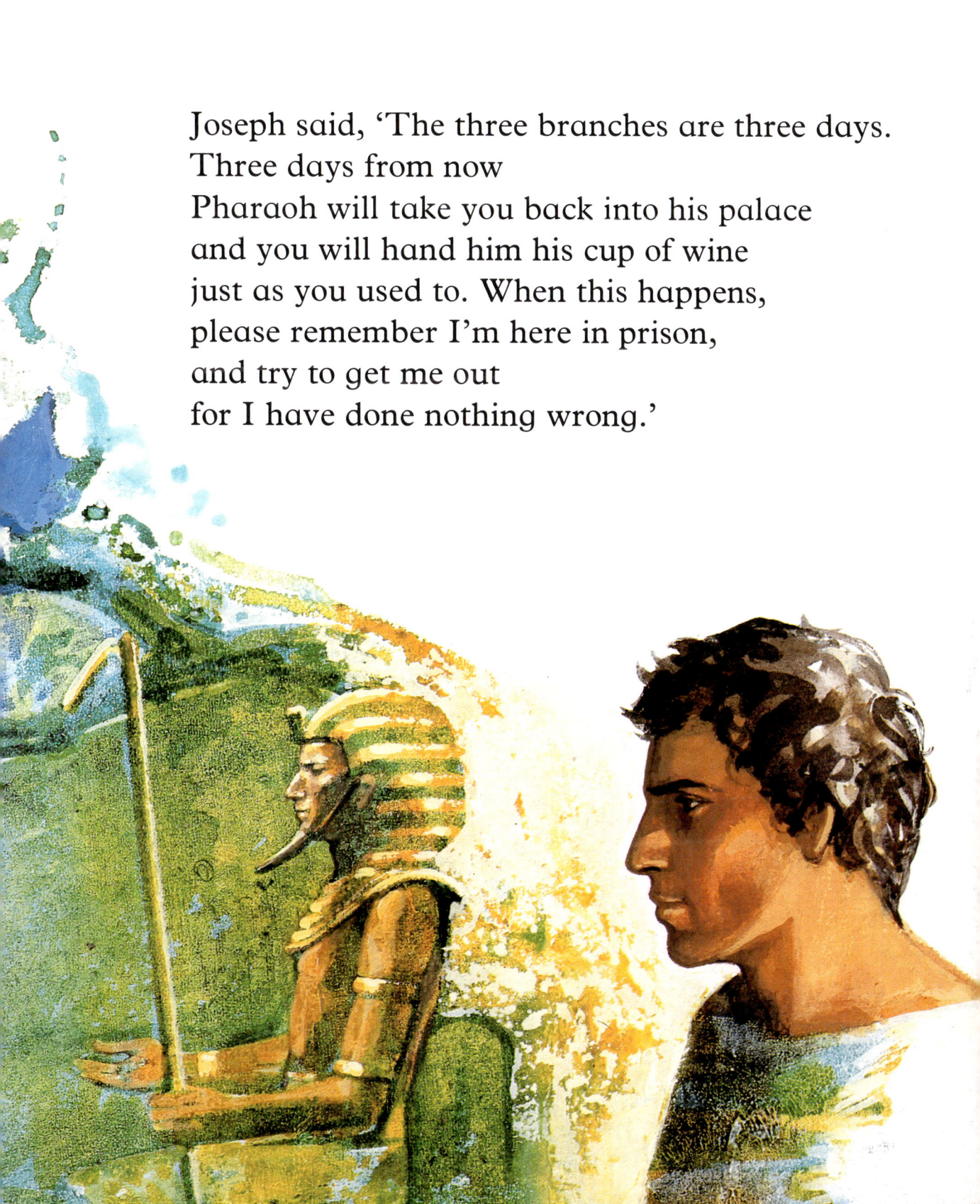

When the baker heard this,
he told Joseph his dream.
'I had three white baskets on my head.

In the top one were all sorts
of baked meats for Pharaoh,
but the birds came and ate them all up.'
Joseph said, 'The three baskets are three days.
In three days' time Pharaoh will hang you.'

What Joseph had said about the dreams came true.
On the third day, Pharaoh sent for the chief butler
to come back to the palace
to take up his old place again.
But when he was there,
the butler forgot all about Joseph.
At the same time, Pharaoh hanged the chief baker.

Two years passed and Joseph was still in prison.
Then one day, Pharaoh dreamed a dream.
He was standing by a river and he saw
seven fat, healthy cattle come up out of the river
and feed in a meadow. Then he saw
seven thin, lean cattle come out of the river
and they ate up the fat cattle.

Then Pharaoh slept and dreamed again.
He saw seven good, plump ears of corn on one stalk.
Then seven thin, miserable ears of corn,
blasted by the east wind,
came and devoured the fat ears.
The next morning Pharaoh was troubled.
He sent for his wise men and magicians,
but none of them could tell him
the meaning of his dreams.

Then at last, the butler remembered Joseph.
He told Pharaoh how Joseph had explained
the meaning of his dream.
Pharaoh sent for Joseph,
who quickly shaved and put on clean clothes
and came out of the prison.
When he heard the dreams, he said to Pharaoh,
'God has shown you what he means to do.'

'The seven cattle and the seven ears of corn are seven years. For the next seven years in Egypt there will be good harvests and plenty of corn. But after that there will be seven years of famine, and people will be very hungry.

Let Pharaoh look for a very wise man,
and set him to govern the land.
Let him make sure that in the seven good years
part of all the corn is stored away.
So then there will be enough food
for the people to eat
when the seven years of famine come afterwards.'

Pharaoh said, 'You have spoken well and wisely.
You shall be the governor
and shall rule Egypt under me.'
Then he took a ring off his own finger
and put it on Joseph's finger.

He gave him a golden chain
and fine linen to wear. For the next seven years
Joseph went round the country,
gathering up more corn than he could count
and saving it for the time of the famine.